Lucien Bély

Professor of the University of Paris – Sorbonne (Paris IV)

The St[illegible] of Les [illegible]x de Pr[illegible]vence

Photographs by Jean-Paul Gisserot
Translated by Angela Caldwell

EDITIONS JEAN-PAUL GISSEROT

The Story of Les Baux de Provence

A look at the chaotic countryside around Les Baux is sufficient to suggest the geological upheavals that created it. Like all the mountains in the limestone region of Provence, it was a twofold thrust from the Alps and Pyrenees that led to the creation of the Alpilles range. The area around Les Baux, on its southern borders, is merely a piece of sandstone that has been sculpted into fantastic shapes by erosion. Rocks have been precariously heaped into a pile. In 1653, the Baumanière Rock crushed a farm and a mill, killing two women and some sheep.

The Baux Plateau stands like the mighty bow of a ship, providing a view of the stony Crau Plain down to Vaccarès and the sea. The Vayède Col separates the spur of rock known as the Bringasses Plateau and Val de la Fontaine (or simply "Val de la Font", Fountain Valley) from the Costapéra Plateau in the west.

The road to Maillane runs through Val d'Enfer (Hell Valley) which may have provided Dante with inspiration for the first poems in his Divine Comedy. The rock falls are certainly impressive enough to inspire such visions. A long time ago, probably in the 1st century B.C, Man cut stone here to build homes. The quarries resemble vast porticos leading nowhere. It was also here, as in Lubéron, that caves gave rise to legends reflecting the age-old fears and fascinations of the shepherds. Perhaps the "Fairy Grotto" (Grotte des Fées or Trau di Fado) is the lair of Taven the Witch, the Baumo de la masco Taven to which Mireille, Mistral's heroine, took Vincent, her wounded friend. The names given to the chambers and abysses in this cave conjure up thoughts of age-old terrors e.g. the Bat (Rato penado), the Black Lamb (Agneu negre), the Nightmare (Chauvovièio), the Exorcism (Escunjur) etc. The cave has everything – ghosts, fantasy spirits, mandrake and the Seven Cats' Pot. Marie Mauron described the world of the caves as underground cities discovered by her heroes in Le sel des pierres by the light of a few matches: "A world of huge hewn blocks of stone, imprisoned water, columns, miniature stalactites, vaulted roofs, avenues and chambers came to life for two or three seconds then faded into darkness as the flame died".

The castle entrance: In Les Baux, the towers like the Saracen's Tower (right) was forward works that defended the citadel.

The first traces of Man

Tombs above the Col de la Vayède, a graveyard well away from the castle and village.

In fact, it was in the Fairy Grotto that flint blades were discovered, with polished stone axes and bone punches, all of which prove that Man was close by two thousand years B.C. in the Chalcolithic Era. Many other later remains show that the people who came to this area were increasingly influenced by the Greek and Roman civilizations. Pottery made from Vayède clay but inspired by Sicilian ceramics, and pottery thought to have been imported were discovered in graveyards, such as the "Catalan" necropolis dating from the 1st century B.C.

Celto-Ligurians sought refuge on the nearby summits close to Les Baux, in particular on the Bringasses Plateau. A citadel was huge walls was built here before the village; it was protected by a moat dug out of the stone and crossed by a bridge. Other similar refuges have been found on the Costapéra Plateau.

Roman civilisation swept right across Provence. The town of Glanum is not far

away. In the 19th century, a stele was discovered at the foot of Les Baux. The three figures carved into it were thought, for many years, to be the legendary three Mary's and a chapel was built in Les Saintes-Maries-de-la-Mer. The name of Trémaïé was given to the figures. In fact, it is probably a much more trivial memorial on which a couple of local worthies had their portraits carved, showing them under the protection of a pagan goddess. Another nearby stele, called Les Gaïé, is said to have been erected by a son in memory of his parents. Then came the early days of Christianity. A strange tradition has it that St. Martin, who evangelised Tours, crossed the Alpilles and the Baux Valley and raised a spring which bears his name.

The Baux lineage : «A Race of Eagles, Vassals Never»

While Cluny Abbey was being founded in Burgundy, Christianity was taking control throughout the Western world. People felt less afraid. In Provence, it was the Archbishops of Arles who embodied the "peace of God". Manassès was one of these powerful, authoritarian priests and he surrounded himself with a few skilful, devoted men. One of them, Isnard, helped by his entire family, was more than willing to take over ecclesiastical estates. He was even excommunicated for his unscrupulously scandalous plundering. Since St. Martin's Abbey in Arles owned an estate in the vallis Felauria, i.e. the Baux Valley, Manassès gave it to his faithful, greedy Isnard between 970 and 978 A.D. A castle was then built on the rocky escarpment.

Landscape around Les Baux.

The much-feared Baux family was founded by Isnard and one of his relatives, Pons "the Ancient", who was a descendent of the mythical Leibulfe, Lord of Argence. With the new dynasty came the legend referred to by Frédéric Mistral at the beginning of his work, Calendal:

"The first, by his ancient name as by his splendour – Great Provencal families – A Race of Eagles, Vassals Never" – Who, with the tip of his wings, - Brushed the crest of all the hills and mountains".

Gradually, the ambitious noblemen accumulated land and honours. Did they actually own seventy-nine estates in Provence, as tradition would have it? Whether or not it was true, tales of this possibly imaginary figure were passed down the generations as if they were historical fact. The family held immense power around Arles where they owned the vast Trinquetaille Castle opposite the old town. In fact, their power and authority spread into the Dauphiné and Comtat Venaissin areas. It was during this period that they began linking their Christian names with their favourite estate, the one that embodied their valour – Les Baux. Balc, which meant "escarpment", became Balchius or Baucius in Latin and the word finally developed its own, provencal form written in many different ways e.g. Baus, Bauz, Baû, until it became Les Baux. It was in the 11th century that Hugues, the younger son of Pons the Younger and Profecta of Marignane, became known as Hugues des Baux. For many years thereafter, members of the family chose the name of other estates but they all felt that they belonged to the same lineage and that individuality was of no real importance. The names of the fearsome barons, their wives or their sisters mattered little; nor did the details of their alliances and descendents. What did matter was a succession of lives and deaths that obeyed only one rule – excess in all things.

The War of Les Baux, the last traces of Provencal feudalism

At the end of the 11th century, a number of families were locked in a tussle to take control of Provence. The Counts of Toulouse were satisfied with a marquisate on the west bank of the River Rhône. Countess Gerberge of Arles, the heir to Provence, eventually married her daughter, Douce, to Raimond-Berenger, Count of Barcelona.

From then on, it was the Catalan prince to whom the lords of Provence paid homage. As to Raimond des Baux, he married Douce's sister Etiennette, which shows the prestige and strength of his name. Raimond provided his lord and brother-in-law with assistance to fight the powerful rebels, the Bruissans; he lent him large sums of money, men and horses. As long as Raimond Berenger ruled, the Baux family did not dispute his power. However, when he died, his wife Etiennette and his sons tried to take control of the entire area of Provence. Faced with the power of the Counts, the Lords of Les Baux decided to act. It was the pride of great noblemen that pushed them to revolt, in the name of feudalism. The "wars of Les Baux" caused bloodshed throughout the county for twenty years and, through the actions of the Baux family, the final hope of an independent principality lived and died.

The castle entrance and the Crau Plain. At the foot of the castle is the "terras" that was traditionally occupied by towns, villages and stables. It was defended by two large towers, the Tour Sarrasine and the Tour des Banes that flanked the Porte de l'Auro, a gate that no longer exists (literally, "Wind Gate").

The huge dynastic claim was, in the end, nothing but an excuse for a revolt.

The Baux family then took the motto: A l'azar, Bautezar, "To chance, Balthazar". A whole lineage looked for a play on the word "Bau ", the embodiment of family destiny. The faithful vassals created the legend that claimed the family was descended from one of the Magi. The 12th century, the time of the Crusades, found these flights of fancy about biblical figures much to its liking. The sixteen-branch star that guided the kings to the stable, the "comet", was placed on the Baux' coat-of-arms which thenceforth became "of gules with one star of sixteen argent branches".

The rebels sought allies and Provence was split. The Count of Toulouse gave them his support but then set off to the Holy Land and left them to their fate. Since Provence was part of the Empire, the Lords of Les Baux turned to the

Top: The bell tower on St. Vincent's Church.
Left: The dovecote in Les Baux. The pigeonholes were dug into the sandstone rock.

Holy Roman Emperor despite the fact that his authority was far away and totally theoretical. It is possible but uncertain whether they corresponded with Conrad but Frederick Barbarossa definitely sent them letters confirming their claims to the County of Provence.

The House of Les Baux, then, rebelled against the Counts of Provence three times and was defeated every time, in an increasingly humiliating way. Raimond of Les Baux died before peace was concluded. By the treaty of 1150, his family had to waive its rights over Provence. After a second unsuccessful rebellion in 1155, Raimond's sons had to open up many of the castles belonging to them. Finally, in 1162, they suffered total defeat and the castle in Les Baux was razed to the ground while its outbuildings were extensively damaged.

From adventure to epic, the glory of the Baux family

The House of Les Baux soon arose from the ashes, however. Its seniority ensured it independence and prestige and it played a central role in plots, revolts and heresies. The ambition of headstrong individuals did the rest. A fine marriage, however, brought the family back to its former glory. Bertrand, Etiennette's third son, married Tiburge, heiress to the principality of Orange. From Emperor Barbarossa, he obtained all the privileges of a great feudal lord. Underlining his honour, he was entitled to ride with banners unfurled; emphasising his power, he was entitled to mint his own coins. In exchange, he had to proclaim himself a soldier of God and, in his prosperity, he was ordered not to forget the Church. He completed the construction of the beautiful Silvacane Abbey which his father had founded. To the Abbey of Saint-Paul-de-Mausole, he gave the Priory of Saint-Vincent-des-Baux. Despite his goodness, however, he was murdered.

Bertrand's three sons (Hugues, Bertrand and Guillaume) founded the dynasty of princes who, by their exploits, complaints and cruelties made the name of Les Baux known throughout Provence and the Christian world. Hugues became Lord of Les Baux; he married the daughter of Barral, Viscount of Marseille, and became his heir. Bertrand, the second son, was made Lord of Berre and the youngest, Guillaume (or William), Prince of Orange. The three branches subdivided again and again, allying themselves with other feudal lineages and sharing out the many estates that belonged to the family.

Most of these knights enjoyed armed combat. Hugues des Baux was an eternal rebel. He revolted against the Count of Provence but the people of Aix handed him over in return for a few pastures and a few areas of woodland. He was released to bring to an end the negotiations between Raymond VII of Toulouse and

Left: The ruins of the old castle, with the keep towering above.

Right: The battlements between the keep and the "Saracen Tower".

the Count of Provence. He argued with the Archbishop of Arles. He even headed a coalition "against all except the Church, the Emperor, the King of France and the people of Arles". All this fighting eventually led to his ruin.

Violence was an integral part of princely life. William of Orange threw himself wholeheartedly into the Albigensian Crusade. He captured the marquisate of Provence in the Pope's name when Raymond VI, Count of Toulouse, was stripped of it after being defeated but William later had to return it to Raymond's son, Raymond VII. The Emperor gave William the title of "King of

Top and bottom: Five views of the mediaeval castle.

Arles", which may have been an honorary title but which nevertheless showed how famous the Prince was. For many years, he continued to support lost causes and he fell into the hands of the heretics in Avignon. Hatred ran so deep that he was skinned alive.

Feudal lords changed sides without giving it a second thought, going where their anger, interest or chance took them. Barral, Hugues' son, began by serving the Count of Toulouse, Raymond VII, becoming his seneschal in the Comtat Venaissin and his nephew through his marriage with Sibylle of Anduze. He fought against Pope Gregory IX and was excommunicated by the Archbishop of Arles, the papal legate. This, however, did not prevent him from winning victory upon victory in Provence. Then, strangely, the nobleman allied himself with the towns of Arles, Avignon and Marseille which, in the name of local freedom, turned themselves into veritable republics, like the Italian towns. Barral became "Podesta" of Avignon. The wind changed direction however. The Lord of Les Baux sent Blanche of Castile a letter in which he prepared to submit to Louis IX's brother, Charles of Anjou, Count of Provence. To gain a pardon and please the King of France, he followed the contemporary ideal, became a Crusader and set off for the Holy Land with a small band of soldiers. On his return, he was made Captain and Grand Judge of the Count of Provence and, acting in his own name, he set off to bring to law and order back to Marseille which was in the grip of revolt and supported by one of his cousins, Hugues des Baux. He also won fame in Italy. His death is the subject of a strange legend. He told his wife, children and leading courtiers about his childhood fear of the crows which he had seen near Saint-Rémy. One of these unlucky birds landed just then on the window of the room in which he was sitting. Barral is said to have dropped dead. Superstition was an integral part of mediaeval faith.

The glory of the Baux family is linked to the fame

of the mediaeval troubadours. They were poets, musicians and singers, many of them noblemen; through the Arts, they injected a degree of humanity and love into a world filled with violence. Frédéric Mistral, who claimed to be a latterday troubadour, described the court of the Baux family in the following terms:

" La pouësio èro tant drudo
La court baussenco tant letrudo
En aquéu tèms ! "

"The poetry was so vigorous
And the Court of Les Baux so well-read
In those days!"

He then listed the troubadours protected by the Lords of Les Baux and the rivalry between the noblemen and poets. Peire Vidal who, according to Mistral, "did a thousand strange things with his she-wolf", was a familiar figure at court. He could never resist a pretty face and he fell in love with Alazaïs de Roquemartine, a member of the Porcelet family and wife of Barral, Viscount of Marseille. He stole a kiss from the beautiful lady while she slept and, out of shame or fear, fled the court. Alazaïs pardoned him, however, at the request of Barral and his son-in-law, Hugues des Baux. The troubadour returned to Provence, having been begged to do so by Dame Alazaïs, and he was welcomed to Marseille by the husband, who bore him no grudge. Fouquet de Marseille also frequented the court of Barral de Marseille. He too loved Alazaïs; in fact when his benefactress died, he entered holy orders. Having become Bishop of Toulouse, he was the tireless enemy of the

The plain to the south of the Alpilles Range, carpeted with olive groves.

Top: Les Baux rock. Mother Nature had already created a citadel.

Bottom: Place Neuve, the square near the Eyguières Gate.

Albigensians, an "abominable" man according to Mistral. He fought side-by-side with Guillaume des Baux, (Prince William of Orange) in the crusade led by Simon de Montfort against the heretics and against his benefactor, the Count of Toulouse. Troubadour Perdigo also accompanied Guillaume and his cousin, Hugues des Baux, praising their "great feats". Gui de Cavaillon, on the other hand, was loyal to the Counts of Toulouse and he launched virulent attacks on the Prince of Orange. The arrogant nobleman claimed to have poetic talents and the poet responded with a play entitled, " Gui à tort me menace " (Gui wrongfully threatens me). His uncle, Raimbaut d'Orange had, after all, been a famous poet, in love with the good Countess of Urgel. A juggler, Raimbaut de Vacqueiras, owed everything to William who raised him to a higher rank and introduced him to aristocratic society in

A view of the Baux Plateau.

Provence. The luxury-loving Barral des Baux gathered to his court a number of poets such as Bertrand d'Alamano, who was always loyal to Charles of Anjou and his lieutenant, Barral. On the other hand, when Marseille rebelled, the warrior was faced not only with his own cousin, Hugues, but also a great troubadour and nobleman, Boniface de Castellane.

Despite their quarrels and hatreds, these rough warriors loved poetry. They enjoyed composing or listening to pastourals, tensons, ballads, sirventes and songs. They crowded to the "Courts of Love" hosted by beautiful ladies. Mistral gave a definition of them in which historic reality is illuminated by legend – they were "poetic assizes in which the most noble and most beautiful ladies, those who were best-versed in "Gay-Saber" (lyric poetry), passed judgement on questions of gallantry and romantic disputes and awarded prizes for Provencal poetry." Many of ladies in the Baux family had this threefold role – a social one since they were central to the aristocratic social life, a moral one since, in the name of love, they settled relationships between people, and finally a literary one since they and others like them inspired all the courtly literature. The chroniclers and especially Jean de Nostradamus in the 16th century have retained a few of the names, among them Clairette des Baux in Signe, Jeanne des Baux in Avignon and Cécile des Baux alias Passe-Rose in Romanin. Mistral also referred to these enchantingly-named ladies who merely provided pretexts for writing and singing:

"Oh! princesses of Les Baux, Huguette, Sibylle, Blanche-Fleur, Baussette -; You who on high had golden rocks for your thrones... The thyme itself has retained the scent – Of your footsteps; and I seem still to see the lively, courtly runners and the bellicose, - That I see at your feet singing like troubadours".

A new land was open to the Provencal lords

in the late 13th century – Italy. The Count of Provence, Charles of Anjou, called his vassals here to provide assistance in his conquest of his kingdom of Naples.

The Lords of Les Baux gained their reputation there. Barral's son Raymond fought at the Battle of Benevento against the legendary Manfred. The noblemen won vast estates and new titles. Barral's descendents became Counts of Avellino, just as their neighbours, descendents of the Lords of Berre, later became Dukes of Andria.

Yet these wandering princes remained closely tied to their birthplace. Raimond was appointed Grand Seneschal of Provence. In fact, they resembled their wild ancestors. Violence occupied their entire life: Raimond, for example, was killed by his own troops when they failed to recognize him during a night-time ambush. They had retained a love of luxury – Barral's other son enjoyed tournaments so much that he spent part of his fortune on them and eventually had to sell Trinquetaille Castle to the Archbishop of Arles.

The Baux family had to impose itself on the Court in Naples, in the face of the king, his family and two branches of the royal blood line, the Duras and the Tarentes. Hugues des Baux became one of King Robert's courtiers, accumulating honours and power e.g. Seneschal of Provence and Grand Admiral of the Kingdom of Naples before becoming Chmaberlain to Queen Joan, the unfathomable, unlucky adventuress, the "bono reino Jano" referred to in tales of Provence. Hugues misused his

St. Blaise' Chapel before restoration.

Pages16 and 17: The White Penitents' Chapel. A secular brotherhood of penitents had this chapel built in the 17th century on Place Saint-Vincent. It was designed so that the bodies of the members of the brotherhood could be buried in its crypt. It lay in ruins in the 20th century but was rebuilt and dedicated to St. Estelle, the patron saint of the Félibrige movement. It was decorated by Yves Brayer who paid homage to the shepherds and scenery of Les Baux in vast frescoes. A low relief has been carved on the West Front showing two penitents in prayer, facing each other. Above them is a round, or bull's eye, window topped by an arcaded bell turret containing a 15th-century bell.

The Taravelle Tower above the dovecote.

powers. He kidnapped Marie, the queen's sister, with the intention of marrying her to his son but the young man raped her. They were sailing to Provence when, during a stopover, Hugues was murdered by Louis de Tarente, the queen's second husband and possibly the murderer of her first spouse. Robert des Baux was taken prisoner and may have been beaten to death by Princess Marie. This was a lineage bathed in tragedy since, at the same time, Izoarde des Baux was burnt at the stake in Romans for having murdered her husband, Pons de Beauvoisin de la Penne.

Dramas continued in Italy and in Provence, while Europe as a whole was struck by two terrible disasters – the Black Death and the Hundred Years War. Robert de Duras captured the citadel at Les Baux by surprise. A few ladders were all that was necessary to capture it during the night. Robert, supported by his uncle, the all-powerful Cardinal de Talleyrand-Périgord, and by all the cardinals, was confronted by three forces i.e. the Pope, Queen Jeanne and, more importantly, Raimond des Baux, Provost of Marseille, whose brother Antoine had been taken prisoner by Robert. The siege lasted for four months. Heavy war machinery, numerous troops and a large sum of money successfully dislodged Robert de Duras, who was killed at the Battle of Poitiers.

The Baux also tried, for reasons of vengeance and ambition, to weaken the House of Tarente. Their ally was Cardinal de Talleyrand

Arriving at Les Baux.

but they were also assisted by outlaw bands known as "grandes compagnies", one of which, led by Archpriest Arnaud de Servole, shook the Avignon papacy to its roots. Amile des Baux took part in the pillaging but law and order was gradually re-establised. The Lords of Les Baux paid dearly for their self-interested involvement. The citadel at Les Baux was besieged and Raimond's assets were confiscated. Pardon was only granted five years later. Raimond's heiress was young Alix. Raymond Roger de Beaufort, Viscount of Turenne, was appointed as her tutor and it was through him that the Baux family were again subjected to a wave of violence in the late 14th century.

Alix' tutor was a leading nobleman. His

Raymond de Turenne, a brigand-lord: "Like a rake with iron teeth"

uncle and great-uncle had both been Popes in Avignon and they had heaped assets on his head. He was an example of papal nepotism. For many years, he was a docile servant. He fought in Flanders for the King of France and in Italy for the Pope. Then, suddenly, he rebelled soon rose up against his awesome father-in-law and signed alliances with all the lord's enemies.

Provence then belonged to the House of Anjou and Queen Marie of Blois reigned there in her son's name. Turenne challenged Marie in 1395, accused her of committing lèse-

The keep.

against all those in power. His entire family, including his mother and his wife, gave him active support and, for some time, he was protected by his illustrious name, his alliances and his power. Despite his countless misdeeds, the princes tried to calm him down and sign ceasefires with him but they were always precarious and always broken. When he looked for a husband for his daughter, there were many candidates – princes of the royal blood coveted the great inheritance. The King of France finally proposed one of his loyal servants, Marshal Boucicaut. However, the son-in-law majesté. He confiscated her assets and placed a price on her head. Nothing, though, would hold this hell-bound lord in check. He also challenged papal authority. The Popes issued excommunications against the shameless brigand, denouncing "this ungrateful son who spits in the face of the Church and the milk suckled at his mother's breast". Cases were taken to trial and he was sentenced to death but he laughed this off. By insolence and bravado, he had the colours of Charles de Durazzo, the rival of the House of Baux, raised on the keep in Les Baux. He also added the colours of the Roman Pope, Boniface IX, rival of Clement VII, Pope in Avignon.

The viscount turned the citadel of Les Baux into his expeditionary centre. According to the Pope, he kept a "band of vile brigands" there, as he did in Castillon and Pertuis, Meyrargues and Les Pennes. The miscreants swept across the plains, robbing merchants as well as travellers, pilgrims and prelates heading for the papal court. After committing their crimes, they would return to their eagle's nests, taking prisoners with them. These prisoners were not released until huge ransoms were paid; in the absence of any ransom, the outlaws threw their unfortunate prisoners off the top of the rock on which Les Baux stands. The pillaging bands attacked towns and villages, spreading fire, rape and death everywhere they went. To be spared such a fate, peasants and burghers would conclude a pact ("patis") with the viscount – and the brigands would acquire wealth from the land. The legend of the "fleou de Provenço", this "Got et cruel Attile" quickly took on more and more detail. Plots were organized to fight him, as described by Mistral in his Nerte: a few barons met with a view to chasing out "The wolves of Raymond de Turenne – You know? the great pillager, - The blackguard, destroyer of monasteries, Who, in his incursions, dragged – Murder and fire and who swept through – Hilltop towns and castles – Like a rake with iron teeth".

After ten years of violence, Turenne, the cynical, bloody noblemen, found himself alone, old and damned, face by countless enemies. His troops abandoned him, his castles fell and he was chased out of Provence. Did he drown or did he die ten years later after obtaining the Church's pardon? History is unsure because the chroniclers were only interested in him as an invincible outlaw.

The Hundred Years War and the pillaging, fighting and black death that followed in its wake, had deeply disturbed people. This led to the appearance of people filled with anger and madness, flamboyant monsters, and Raymond, "this enemy of the human soul and body" may well have been a precursor of Gilles de Rais, Joan of Arc's companion who turned into a bloodthirsty brute.

Once her tutor had been defeated, Alix des

Numerous cave dwellings have been dug into the rock face at Les Baux.

The King of France, protector of Les Baux

Baux regained her assets. Literature has described this woman, the final embodiment of the great Provencal family, as a serene, peaceful person. They show her protecting the precious, rare springs and water that flowed across her lands to Carpentras. In her will, where she described her famous castle in great detail, she bequeathed her estate in Les Baux to her distant cousin, the Duke of Andria. Yolande of Aragon, widow of the Count of Provence, found this unacceptable, besieged the town and captured it. After all, could a monarch not take back what he or she had granted in previous times? Les Baux was lost to the family with the illustrious name – this was the first time the citadel was subject to outside authority.

Having been "annexed" to the County of Provence, the Baux estate was inherited by René of Anjou, known as "Good King René". His wife, Jeanne of Laval, liked this Provencal residence and set about improving it. René, a cultured, human prince, granted the people of Les Baux rights and privileges which made their everyday lives much easier. From then on, the village of Les Baux held greater sway than the citadel and a certain gentle lifestyle replaced the roughness of feudal times.

On the death of René and his heir, Charles of Maine, Provence fell into the hands of King Louis XI of France. This was the second period of sub-

Keeping watch over the plain.

A squinch on a staircase.

jection for Les Baux. Palamède de Forbin, Lieutenant-General of the province, wanted to demolish the town walls around Les Baux but the death of the king halted the project. It was, however, no more than a brief interlude. The lordly estate of Les Baux became a barony and was granted to the king's loyal servants. The first of them was Brother Bernardin, a knight of the Order of St. John of Jerusalem, famous for his exploits as a "Great Privateer" and a courtier to King Louis XII. Then came François I's childhood friend, Constable Anne de Montmorency. During his time in Provence, the fearsome, pitiless warrior successfully repulsed a dangerous attempt at invasion on the part of Emperor Charles V.

Out of friendship and gratitude, King

Luxury and fear in the shadow of beautiful Renaissance residences

François I paid a visit to the fortress at Les Baux, in which the Constable had retrenched his troops. Since the Middle Ages, such an official visit to a town had been used as an excuse to put the royal personage in the spotlight and stage sumptuous festivities. The people of Les Baux showed their allegiance to the king. In exchange, the sovereign and suzerain was expected to heap benefits on the townspeople. François I did just that.

Early in the 16th century, Anne de Montmorency introduced new architectural and decorative fashions into Provence. They came straight from Italy. A number of powerful families, the Brions and Porcelets, all of them allied to each other, commissioned the building of superb mansions. The town took on a whole new appearance. Claude de Manville, who commanded the fortress in the Baron's absence, was admired and respected. He made his family's fortune, as is evident from the beautiful residence built for his nephew by Flayelle, an architect from the Vivarais area. Wide windows replaced the narrow mediaeval slit windows, letting light flood into vast chambers that contained monumental fireplaces. The town's streets were lined by these tall houses with beautiful Italianate façades which still bear the names of their splendid owners e.g. Jean Manson the Elder, Nicolas Martel and Brisson-Peyre. It was the bourgeoisie which dazzled, not the feudal Baux family.

Towards the end of the 16th century came the Wars of Religion and they caused disorder in Les Baux. The Reformed Religion was to make great strides in the town and passionate arguments broke out. Supporters of Protestantism seized the castle and threw the relics from St. Catherine's Chapel (which they considered as signs of superstition) into a well. The Manville family soon took up the new religion and a Protestant church was set up in

The Porcelets' mansion.

A village street.

one of the outbuildings of their mansion. The "religionnaries'" motto, Post tenebras lux ("After the darkness, the light") was engraved on the pediment above one of the windows which was restored in the 19th century. Jeanne de Quiqueran, wife of Montmorency's successor, was also converted to Protestantism. She and her sister, Marguerite, had a hospital built at the top of the town, near the old St. Blaise' Chapel. It cared for ordinary patients and St. Andrew's Hospital in the valley was turned into a leper hospital. The famous "Queen Jeanne's Pavilion" in the Font Valley was also built for Jeanne de Quiqueran and is a Renaissance gem.

Yet it was her nephew who led the fight against the Protestant "heresy" and, in 1619, a Protestant preacher was run out of Les Baux; he was only able to preach in Maussane, at Manville Mill. A tragic accident occurred at that time. The Chevalier de Lorraine, brother of the Duke de Guise, paid a visit to Les Baux. Anxious to show off his skills, he let off an old cannon and was fatally wounded when the gun exploded.

Although the town prospered during the 16th century, despite internal divisions, the citadel was nevertheless regarded with mistrust by the monarch's representatives.

Richelieu, the all-powerful minister to Louis

In the name of the king, the citadel, the symbol of independence, is demolished

XIII, cunningly attacked the ramparts which, all over France, seemed to be thumbing their noses at royal authority and those who represented it in the name of local liberty. A complex operation, which had secretly been prepared a long time before, was instigated against the Baux family. The Baron des Baux, Antoine de Villeneuve, courtier to Gaston d'Orléans, Louis' enemy brother, was called to the court. During his absence, a captain was sent to occupy the town. The local people resisted a siege that did not dare to call itself that for one month but they eventually realized that their fate was sealed and that the king's orders would have to be carried out.

The town gates were opened and the town walls were demolished. A master mason from Tarascon, accompanied by colleagues from Marseille, won the contract for the work and they demolished the ramparts using gunpowder and picks. This was the final period of subjection for Les Baux. It marked the end of the castle, the end of a legend and the end of warfare. It also marked the decline of the Baux family which, deprived of their military vocation, lost their reason to live.

Louis XIII toyed with the town. The local population had to buy their own town back from the monarch. To pay the enormous sum demanded, they acquired debts, especially as they were also required to provide the upkeep of the troops who ensured law and order. Eleven years later, obsessed by the complaints and pleas, King Louis XIII offered to

Jean de Brion's mansion.

Queen Joan's Pavilion.

An impregnable town?

repurchase the town and paid back the money he had received. Les Baux became a "royal town" but it was a town without a soul.

The king used it as an item for exchange. In 1641, the young Prince of Monaco had the gates of his town opened to French troops and they routed the Spanish garrison that was occupying the town, having been called there by the prince's tutor and uncle. As the lands owned by the Prince of Monaco outside France risked confiscation by the Spaniards, the estates of Les Baux and Saint-Rémy were given to him by the King of France in compensation. Hercule Grimaldi then became "Marquis of Les Baux" by royal order.

What kings had begun, the passing years completed. Security improved and made the rocky refuge unnecessary. The marshes in the plains were drained. Soon, people preferred to live in the hamlets of Maussane, Mouriès and Saint-Martin-de Castillon in the plain.

The French Revolution exacerbated the

In the kingdom of "glittering death"

opposition between Les Baux and the low-lying lands round about. When the priest in Les Baux, supported by the monarchist population, refused to take an oath in favour of a civil constitution for the clergy, he had to hide and he was eventually deported. Meanwhile, the priest in Maussane, on the other hand, was encouraged by the Republicans and declared his support for the new regime. The disorder worsened. The Mayor, who stood up

The Porcelets' mansion.

«Pénitents Blancs» chapel.

to a former brigand, now a supporter of the Revolution, was coldbloodedly stabbed to death. The peasants took over the castle and burnt all the charters there, seeing them as symbols of their social humiliation.

To calm the situation, the hamlets were turned into independent towns. Les Baux, isolated and but a shadow of its former self, began to lose its population. Houses were gradually abandoned. Yet a scientific discovery drew

1 

 2

1 : The Eyguières Gate, at the end of the Eyguières road. It was protected by a guardrail battlements and the porter's house.. **2 :** The Manville funereal chapel. **3 :** St. Vincent's Church.

attention to a town that had become a village. A chemist named Berthier observed, circa 1821, the properties of a red rock which was named after the village where it had been found – it was "bauxite". The stone was used to extract alumina and make aluminium. Leading scientist Sainte-Claire Deville perfected the production of the new, precious metal. The world was entering the industrial age.

Ruins, though, continued to take over Les Baux, turning it into the kingdom of "glittering death", as it was so prettily described by Marie Mauron.

Les Baux enjoyed a rebirth because this

 3

major mediaeval town was celebrated by Frédéric Mistral. He was, after all, born in the "judge's house" in Maillane, which had a view of the Alpilles. This was his homeland. Even when a child, Mistral enjoyed legends. In the first pages of his Memoirs, he talked about the princes of Les Baux whose citadels sat atop the hills, the ladies in their Courts of Love who sleep in the depths of the valleys and the fairies that haunt the caves in "Hell Valley". Young Mistral attracted a number of writers who wanted to rediscover the sources of inspiration of the mediaeval troubadours, to save the Provencal language. This gave rise to the Félibrige, from a beautiful, forgotten name in mediaeval songs. It was a strong reaction movement. The constant, tireless efforts of educators and administrators to impose a national (i.e. Parisian) culture on France as a whole threatened all the Provencal traditions. Mistral and his friends were passionate about history, costumes and the tales of their province and Provençal was the instrument they used to put them to music.

Post tenebras lux, 1571 – "After the darkness, light" was a motto, a "slogan", a rallying cry for supporters of the Reformed Religion who were not yet "Protestants" but, in the "Roman Catholic" view, merely heretics. The Reformation had great success in Les Baux where it was accepted by the town's richest families. Under the terms of the Reformed Religion, the warring papacy, lazy monks, superstition and trade in indulgences constituted "darkness". The Reformation, on the other hand, marked a rebirth of Christianity. The "Protestant church" was installed in an outbuilding of the Manville family's residence and was, therefore, a "private" place protected by the prestige of this high-ranking dynasty.

Mistral's entire work is rooted in the area of Les Baux. In Mirèio, which inspired Gounod to write an opera, a young girl sings of the beauty of the castle ruins in Les Baux: "I would turn Les Baux into my capital – On the rock where today it clambers – I would rebuild our old ruined castle – and I would add a turret which, with its white tip, - Would reach the stars!".

Calendal (Calendau in Provencal) begins with a melancholic tale of a princess from Les Baux who exalts the past glory of her ancestors and their glory now they are dead: "Now, in the shadows of the chapels – Where nobody in the world remembers them, - Beneath the inscribed flags, they sleep, stretched out on their backs – And, hands clasped, the pellitory – Now dressed from top to bottom – In their old keep, now groans – The sad owl, where could be heard the sound – Of the mandora. "

While Mistral enjoyed national, or even international, adulation, receiving the Nobel Prize for Literature in 1904, a poet and peasant named Charles Rieu, hardly ever left the

Baux area. To quote Mistral, he was the "only man in France to sing of his plough and to do it successfully", in his Chansons du terroir (Songs of the Earth). Rarely was there a writer closer to the soil and the people who hummed his songs. Marie Mauron mentioned the "troubadour of the Paradou area" and, through him, the world of shepherds and their age-old customs.

Since the 16th century, it would appear

The offering of the Christmas lamb – Xmas in Les Baux

that a number of customs have survived , despite warnings and condemnations from the Church, through the strange "Brotherhood of Shepherds of Les Baux" (confrérie des bergers baussencs).

Christmas is their feast day. The sacred blends with good humour, mystery combines with poetry. The "shepherds from Gap" and the "shepherds from Les Baux, all men with common sense", as Charles Rieu calls them in a Christmas song, turned Christmas Eve into a morning concert. The shepherds' songs are the result of solitude. An illiterate man from Romanin used to come and tell the shepherds a "bizarre tune in which the real was more real than a dream" (Marie Mauron). The shepherds sing, "We have come down, the shepherds of the mountain – To announce that Christmas is approaching".

The shepherds must offer a "calendal", or "Christmas", lamb to God. It is laid in a small decorated cart drawn by a ram complete with bells and red pompoms. A procession follows, with cymbals, flutes and tambourines, to the

The town of Les Baux.

Church of St. Vincent. During Midnight Mass, for which all the local people climb up to Les Baux, there is a true mediaeval "mystery" in which each gesture is regulated by tradition and in which cherubs, shepherds and shepherdesses all have a part to play. When the Agnus Dei is heard, the lamb's tail is pinched so that it bleats three times. This ceremony confirms the permanence of the customs of Les Baux that the poets tried so hard to preserve.

It was the poets who, by singing princes and troubadours, revived the old glory of Les Baux. Artists settled here, among them Louis Jou in Jean de Brion's house and, later, another engraver called François de Hérain.

A whole panoply of arts and crafts is coming back to life in the shadow of the old town. Jou attracted writer André Suarez here and he had himself buried in the communal graveyard, at the top end of the town. Les Baux then enjoyed a cultural and artistic revival just as its natural beauty and its legends began to attract travellers.

The ruins have their own secret charm. It is

There are shadows wandering through the sun-drenched streets

the charm that grips Angélique, one of Marie Mauron's heroines, when she sees a few photographs. "They were photographs of bare, tortured hills, a village perched at the end of a spur of rock, piles of rocks and ruins, a flock of sheep among the ruins; the entrance to a quarry looking like an Egyptian temple, then yet more ruins including demolished houses with no roofs, ribbed vaulting collapsing onto wild figs and watched over by black cypress, parapet walkways, slit windows overrun with ivy and blackberries, arches, a keep, tombs, a turret – then the postern gate for a town in which the broken battlements sag beneath the weight of a lotus tree with twenty branches. The same ruins inspired René Char, the poet from the Sorgue, in his Bulletin des Baux : "The ruins, steeped in the uture, the ruins that were inconsistent before you arrived, happy man, go from their plots of land to your love". These piles of rocks reflect the fearsome fragility of human ambitions and constructions. What had once been the pride of the mediaeval noblemen (the citadel) and the pride of the Renaissance middle classes, the town with its beautiful house front has been retuned to a period in which nature reigns. The sun and rain have worn away this inexplicable, fearsome, fantastic sight. Yet the ruins prove and demonstrate the splendour of the past, giving the men of action and war of days gone by, through dialogue with men of action and warriors, giving them a chance to establish an identity for the knights and dreamers, troubadours and poets, in fact the most previous and mysterious part of identity - memory.

The Charloun Rieu memorial on the plateau in Les Baux.

Back cover: the Manville Residence. The village of Les Baux.